# DINOSAUR HUNTERS

## BY CATHERINE CHAMBERS

guin
dom
se

RK,
ND DELHI

**DK DELHI**
Editor Pomona Zaheer
Assistant Art Editor Radhika Kapoor
Designers Sachin Gupta, Syed Md. Farhan
Picture Researcher Aditya Katyal
Managing Editor Soma B. Chowdhury
Managing Art Editor Ahlawat Gunjan
nt

Subject Consultant
David Christensen

With special thanks to Daniel Brinkman and Jacques Gauthier,
Vertebrate Paleontology Division, Yale Peabody Museum of Natural History

First published in Great Britain by
Dorling Kindersley Limited
80 Strand, London, WC2R 0RL

Copyright © 2015 Dorling Kindersley Limited
A Penguin Random House Company
10 9 8 7 6 5 4 3 2 1
001—270531—January/2015
All rights reserved.
Without limiting the rights under copyright reserved above, no part of this publication
may be reproduced, stored in or introduced into a retrieval system, or transmitted,
in any form, or by any means (electronic, mechanical, photocopying, recording, or
otherwise), without the prior written permission of the copyright owner.

A CIP catalogue record for this book is available
from the British Library.

ISBN: 978-0-24118-259-8

Printed and bound in China by South China Printing Company.

The publisher would like to thank the following for
their kind permission to reproduce their photographs:
(Key: a-above; b-below/bottom; c-centre; f-far; l-left; r-right; t-top)

**4 Dreamstime.com**: Vladyslav Starozhylov (br/Cell phone). **Fotolia**: Scanrail (crb/Picture Globe). **5 Fotolia**: Scanrail (tl, cr, clb). **8 Corbis**: photonewzealand / Miz Watanabe. **10 Getty Images**: Stone / Ryan McVay. **12 Mark Ryan**. **12–13 Getty Images**: UIG via Getty Images (Dinosaur background). **13 Alamy Images**: Blaine Harrington III. **15 Getty Images**: Digital Vision / Jim Jordan Photography. **18 Alamy Images**: Niday Picture Library. **20 Corbis**: Siede Preis. **24 Alamy Images**: GL Archive (cla, bl). **24–25 Getty Images**: UIG via Getty Images (Dinosaur background). **26 Alamy Images**: Heritage Image Partnership Ltd. (cra). **26–27 Alamy Images**: Heritage Image Partnership Ltd. (cb). **Getty Images**: Siede Preis (Dinosaur background). **27 Alamy Images**: Heritage Image Partnership Ltd (cla, t, br). **29 Alamy Images**: ClassicStock. **32–33 Corbis**: Jim Smithson (t). **35 Alamy Images**: RWP Photography / Rick Pisio. **37 Corbis**: Bettmann (br). **38–39 Dorling Kindersley**: The Science Museum, London (Locomotive). **Getty Images**: UIG via Getty Images (Dinosaur background). **40–41 Alamy Images**: UIG via Getty Images (Dinosaur background). **40 Dorling Kindersley**: The Science Museum, London (c). **42–43 Getty Images**: UIG via Getty Images (Dinosaur background). **43 Getty Images**: (t). **44–45 Alamy Images**: Stephen Saks Photography (b). **49 Corbis**: Bettmann (br). **50 Alamy Images**: Arletta Cwalina. **52 Alamy Images**: whiteboxmedia limited. **53 Corbis**: 2 / Caroline Woodham / Ocean. **54–55 Dreamstime.com**: Rangizzz (Magazine). **Getty Images**: UIG via Getty Images (Dinosaur background). **55 Getty Images**: (t). **56–57 Getty Images**: UIG via Getty Images (Dinosaur background). **58–59 Getty Images**: UIG via Getty Images (Dinosaur background). **58 Alamy Images**: North Wind Picture Archives (l). **The Bridgeman Art Library**: Peter Newark Western Americana / Private Collection / American School (19th century) (r). **61 Alamy Images**: GREG RYAN. **62–63 Alamy Images**: Clint Farlinger. **65 Corbis**: Bettmann (br). **69 Dreamstime.com**: Maksym Yemelyanov (Mobile); Troyka (Whirl background). **70–71 Getty Images**: UIG via Getty Images (Dinosaur background). **70 Alamy Images**: Photocuisine (cr). **71 Corbis**: Envision (bl). **72–73 Getty Images**: UIG via Getty Images (Dinosaur background). **76–77 Alamy Images**: Stephen Saks Photography. **78 Dreamstime.com**: Kmitu (c/Paper). **80 Alamy Images**: National Geographic Image Collection. **82 Corbis**: Richard T. Nowitz. **83 Corbis**: Bettmann (br). **84 Dreamstime.com**: Yanta (reproduced four times on page 84–85). Image courtesy of Biodiversity Heritage Library. http://www.biodiversitylibrary.org: The life of a fossil hunter, by Charles H. Sternberg (c). **TopFoto.co.uk**: The Granger Collection (crb). **84–85 Getty Images**: UIG via Getty Images (Dinosaur background). **85 University of Kansas Natural History Museum**: (crb). **86–87 Getty Images**: UIG via Getty Images (Dinosaur background). **87 Dorling Kindersley**: State Museum of Nature, Stuttgart (tr). **88–89 Getty Images**: UIG via Getty Images (Dinosaur background). **91 Corbis**: All Canada Photos / Stephen J. Krasemann. **92 Alamy Images**: nik wheeler. **95 Corbis**: Visuals Unlimited / Albert Copley (cra/Dinosaur skull). **Dreamstime.com**: Maksym Yemelyanov (r). **97 Corbis**: Ocean / Richard Nowitz / 167. **98–99 Alamy Images**: Robert Harding Picture Library Ltd. **100–101 Corbis**: Aurora Photos / Carl D. Walsh. **101 Alamy Images**: Phil Degginger (tr). **Reuters**: Tomas Bravo (MEXICO ENVIRONMENT SOCIETY) (tl). **102–103 Getty Images**: UIG via Getty Images (Dinosaur background). **102 Getty Images**: CSA Images (cla). **105 Corbis**: Eric Nguyen. **108 Alamy Images**: Yury Zap (Book Under Cover). **Corbis**: Bettmann (Cover). **110–111 Alamy Images**: H. Mark Weidman Photography. **112 Alamy Images**: Stefan Sollfors. **114–115 Getty Images**: UIG via Getty Images (Dinosaur background). **116–117 Getty Images**: UIG via Getty Images (Dinosaur background). **117 Corbis**: Bettmann (cl). **Getty Images**: UIG via Getty Images (clb, bl). **119 Alamy Images**: All Canada Photos. **122–123 Getty Images**: UIG via Getty Images (Dinosaur background).

**Jacket images: Front: Corbis**: Corbis: Jim Smithson (Background). **Dorling Kindersley**: American Museum of Natural History (c)

All other images © Dorling Kindersley
For further information see: www.dkimages.com

Discover more at.
**www.dk.com**

# CONTENTS

# MEET THE MEMBERS

Secretly Living in the Past, or SLIP, is an unusual history club. Together, its members decided to buy a commercial mobile app that accessed online excursions of museums and historical sites around the world. However, these app users experimented with the app and came across an exciting function: the app allowed them to be physically transported to historical and archaeological sites. In their first adventure, Seth discovered an even more amazing function on the app – one that enabled them all to tumble back in time, to face history as it happened.

SECRETLY LIVING IN THE PAST

**Seth:** from a farm in Cornwall, England. He is an app expert and inventor. Seth discovered, really by accident, how to SLIP into the past. This development took him on SLIP's very first expedition to ancient Rome.

**Luana:** from São Pedro da Aldeia in Brazil. She is interested in ancient religions, cultures and customs. She developed an app that explains local religions and customs in any location or time period to SLIP members on a mission.

**Hiroto:** from Kyoto in Japan. He is passionate about languages, both ancient and modern. He has developed a translator app and was crucial to the success of the first SLIP expedition. He is also vital to operations, usually monitoring each SLIP from his home base in Kyoto. He has saved many a mission.

# THE LOCATION

Let's slip back to the Wild West, to Wyoming in the year 1890. It is a time of great progress in the United States of America, when the telegraph was just beginning to give way to the telephone. It was when electric power was lighting up cities and transforming lives. On the prairies and in the mountains, however, it was a different story. There were still cowboys and railway builders, trekkers and gold diggers – and dinosaur hunters. For while much of America was powering forwards into the future, there were people determined to unearth its past.

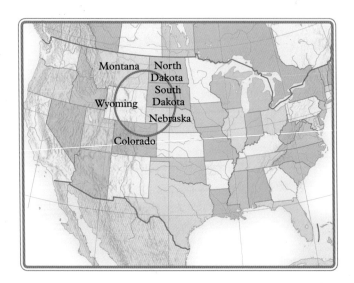

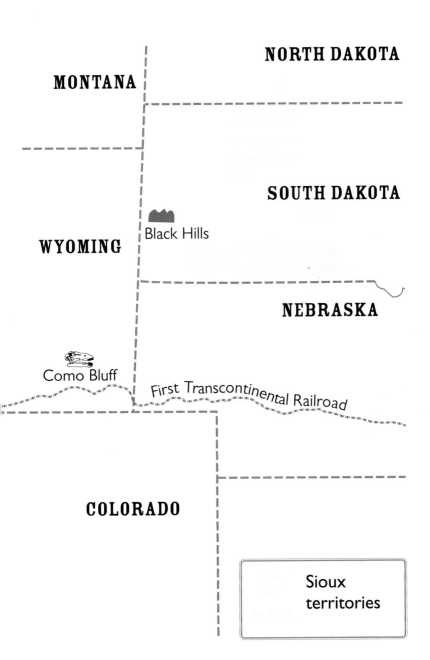

NORTH DAKOTA

MONTANA

SOUTH DAKOTA

Black Hills

WYOMING

NEBRASKA

Como Bluff

First Transcontinental Railroad

COLORADO

Sioux
territories

# PROLOGUE

Seth stood at the farm gate, watching his parents' car as it disappeared towards the morning sun. They were leaving early to go to a sheep auction and would not be back until late. Perfect! Seth wandered past a field of ancient standing stones, where archaeologists had recently come to seek answers.

Seth was so excited that history was being discovered on his own doorstep. Then an even greater thrill overwhelmed him. He was going on a SLIP!

Seth raced back to the farmhouse and checked his mobile. Ten minutes to go. He and Luana were going to be sucked back into the late-19th century, to the Wild West and the gold-rush town of Deadwood in the Black Hills of South Dakota – or were they?

Seth started dreaming of other landing sites. Maybe he would rather join the dinosaur-fossil hunters on Como Bluff in Wyoming. Hmmm. Chunks of gold or hunks of dinosaur? Seth couldn't decide. He copied the app and started working on some new coordinates. Of course, he and Luana had only researched the history of Deadwood in detail, and they didn't know much about dinosaur hunters in Wyoming.

Across the Atlantic in Brazil, Luana hastily finished writing an e-mail to her grandma.

"I'll visit you soon, Grandma. I'd love to hear more of your old tales some time. It's just that I'm a bit busy for now. Love, Luana xx."

She signed off and rapidly texted Seth, "Seth! R U ready 2 SLIP? It's nearly time! I don't have a landing app! Where is it?"

Seth panicked, his fingers fumbling. He sent the app and time-synchronised his phone with Luana's – just 20 seconds to go. Phew! Now 5 – 4 – 3 – 2 – 1. He pressed the launch keys: star – hash – hash – hash.

As Seth lifted his thumb from the last hash key, he realised that they were travelling on the wrong app, the one he had been working on. He had not even perfected any landing coordinates! They could touch down anywhere! In the nanosecond he had left to think or feel before plunging into the unknown, Seth shook with fear. It was not so much that he didn't have a clue where he was going. It was much, much worse than that. It was the thought of having to face Luana.

# Wild West Tours

## MAIN ATTRACTION: DINOSAUR BONES!

A desolate, windblown ridge overlooking the rolling hills of the High Plains of Wyoming

**History:** In 1877, William Harlow Reed, a worker on the Union Pacific Railroad, discovered a treasure trove of dinosaur fossils on the steep north side of the ridge of Como Bluff. By 1889, these fossils were the focus of a fierce competition among fossil hunters, which was known as the Bone Wars.

## MAIN ATTRACTION:
## GOLD!

A lively gold-rush town in
the sacred Black Hills of
South Dakota

**History:** In 1874, a government expedition
found gold in the Black Hills, a place that is
sacred for the Lakota people and was promised
to them by a treaty. The government tried to
keep the discovery secret, but soon the Black
Hills Gold Rush was on. To this day, the Lakota
are still trying to get the land back.

# CHAPTER 1

———◦∞∞◦———

# NO GOLDEN LANDING

THUMP! Seth landed awkwardly on top of a box covered with a dusty canvas tarpaulin. THUD! Luana landed on top of Seth. She caught her breath and brushed down her clothes.

"Seth! You gave me exactly the same coordinates as you gave yourself, and we've landed in the same place!" she snapped.

"Uh, yes. Sorry. Actually, Luana, you see I hadn't quite finished the coordinates. In fact, it's not actually the right version of the app. Actually..."

"If you say 'actually' one more time, I'm going home!" Luana scanned the landscape quickly as she spoke, and sniffed the air – she smelled dust, wild plants and the earthiness of animals. To the right, tall wooden warehouses cast early-morning shadows over goods piled high outside massive doorways. Farmhands hauled them inside, shouting, whistling and laughing as they worked. Horse-drawn wagons clattered in from farms set deep into the countryside, lurching with the weight of cowhides, sheep's wool, dried meat, fresh meat and grain. The horses, gleaming from beads of sweat rolling down their necks, bowed their heads low into cool drinking troughs.

To the left, a train steamed up a shimmering railway track snaking into the distance. Spread out ahead, vast, dusty prairies seemed to move, their seas of dried grasses swaying in the warm breeze. Tiny jewels of red, blue and gold flowers nodded among them, while hawks circled in the distance over grazing cattle. Luana and Seth stood still, awed by the landscape's wild beauty.

"This isn't Deadwood," Seth observed.

"You don't say!"

"I know this isn't the bustling town you expected, but I think those are the Black Hills in the distance. Maybe we could hitch a ride? Find some old-timers? Record a few great stories?" Seth's voice trailed off.

"Okay, Seth. So what went wrong?"

"The thing is, Luana, I was messing around with a copy of the app. I thought we might want a change of plan – maybe land on a ranch, or in the middle of Como Bluff? You know – where they dug up dinosaur fossils?"

"Well, really, Seth!" Then, in her usual practical manner, she said, "Not much we can do about it now. Let's just try to see what history we can get while we're here, even though we're not prepared. Those farmhands and cowboys must have some great tales to tell, and look at this poster on the shed door! It says, 'Buffalo Bill's Wild West and Congress of Rough Riders of the World. Buffalo Bill will appear at every performance'. Seth! It's the Wild Westers – Buffalo Bill and the Lakota Sioux performers! They travel all over the USA and Europe putting on displays of horsemanship and lassoing, and spiritual dances."

"Fantastic!" exclaimed Seth. "Maybe I can record some Lakota tales."

"And I might get an insight into their spirit world," Luana replied. "Now that's really my thing!"

She bent down to brush the dust off her neat, buttoned ankle boots and noticed some writing on a box.

"Look, Seth! What's this?"

They dragged the tarpaulin covering it onto the ground and read out names and addresses, one set painted in black and the other in red.

"It says here, 'For the attention of Edward Drinker Cope, Academy of Natural Sciences, Philadelphia'. On the other side, it says 'URGENT! KEEP OUT! The property of Othniel Charles Marsh, Yale Peabody Museum of Natural History'."

"Wow! Edward Cope and Othniel Marsh, the famous dinosaur-fossil hunters!" Seth said. "I wonder which one this box belongs to. It can't be both. They weren't exactly the best of friends. Dinosaur hunting in these times wasn't called the 'Bone Wars' for nothing."

Luana and Seth looked at each other and then at the box. Each knew exactly what the other was thinking.

URGENT!
KEEP OUT!
The Property of
Othniel Charles Marsh

"Well, if we don't open it, we won't have a hope of sending it to the right palaeontologist," said Luana. "If we take a picture of its contents and send it to Hiroto, he might be able to identify it – and its owner – for us. The trouble is, he's on holiday. Let's face it – that's why we chose this mission. We knew we wouldn't need him to help with any language problem in the USA. Still, we can try to contact him."

"You're right. You know, Luana, I think our mission to get these bones to their destination was supposed to happen."

"Hmmm. Possibly. Come on then. Let's open the box. HEAVE!"

Once the dust had cleared, they peered down.

"It's a dinosaur head!" yelled Luana and Seth together, grinning with delight.

Seth lifted it carefully and set it down on the ground.

The curious but perfectly fossilised skull was shaped like a long box, with a mouth that looked like a smiling zipper and two nostrils on its flat top. Seth and Luana walked around it, hastily snapping images with their mobiles and sending them straight to Hiroto with a message.

"Hi, Hiroto. We know u r on holiday. But u r in New York! So could u identify this 4 us please? From the museum? And tell us who dug it up?"

"Waaaaa! Waooo!"

Two Lakota Sioux raced towards Seth and Luana and seized them by the arms. Their belts were strung with beaded tassels, weapons and tools that rattled against their buffalo-skin clothes. Luana and Seth felt the ground tremble beneath their feet as a Lakota posse rode in on horseback to support the two men.

"Let's SLIP!" yelled Luana.

"We... we can't," replied Seth, his heart racing. "Because..."

Seth's throat closed then, and the words just would not come. He looked up into the pale-blue sky, hoping that help would fall from it. All he saw was a scary but magnificent bald eagle circling.

# COPE v MARSH

It is the great scientific battle of the century: Edward Drinker Cope versus Othniel Charles Marsh. Which palaeontologist will be the victor?

**Edward Drinker Cope**

**Origin:** Philadelphia, Pennsylvania, USA
**Born:** 28 July, 1840
**Age:** 50
**Affiliation:** Academy of Natural Sciences
**Years active:** 1864–1897
**Dinosaurs discovered:** 56
**Major discoveries:** *Camarasaurus, Coelophysis, Dimetrodon*

**Othniel Charles Marsh**

**Origin:** Lockport, New York, USA
**Born:** 29 October, 1831
**Age:** 59
**Affiliation:** Yale Peabody Museum of Natural History
**Years active:** 1866–1899
**Dinosaurs discovered:** 80
**Major discoveries:** *Allosaurus, Diplodocus, Stegosaurus*

## COPE:

Mr Marsh has continually tried to discredit and insult me.
Since 1870, when I discovered the *Elasmosaurus*, he has
done everything in his power to make a fool of me. It is
he who should be scorned – for putting the *Camarasaurus*
head on the *Apatosaurus* body!

## MARSH:

Ha! I hardly need to 'try' to discredit Mr Cope.
He does much of the work all on his own. You see,
the *Elasmosaurus*, as Cope calls it, is not a 'plated reptile',
as the name suggests, but rather a 'twisted reptile'.
'*Steptosaurus*' is a much more accurate name. If he had
not put the vertebrae in back-to-front, with the head
on the wrong end, he might have known that.

## COPE:

Well, at least I haven't been stealing other people's ideas.
I know Marsh has been spying on me. I have heard that
your man Reed has been poking around my quarries!

## MARSH:

Preposterous! Why would I need to stoop to such depths?
If anyone has been stealing, it is Cope – he has been
taking fossils and employees from me since the beginning.
I hope he enjoys working with that traitor Carlin! I know
Cope has been coming to my lectures and then publishing
my theories himself, too!

## COPE:

How dare he! My ideas are all original. I do not need
to bother with Marsh's half-baked theories. In time,
the world will recognise how wrong he is.

# A Day in the Life of a Lakota Sioux

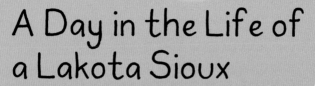

My name is Wapasha, or Red Leaf. My father is Matoska, or White Bear, and my mother is Ojinjintka, or Rose. Our people, the Lakota, follow the buffalo, so we are always on the move. Come and join me for a day!

SUNRISE: It is the first day at our new camp. We arrived yesterday after following the buffalo here. It is time for breakfast of wojapi (berry pudding) and buffalo pemmican (dried meat with cherries).

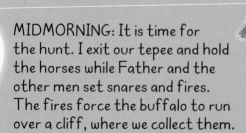

MIDMORNING: It is time for the hunt. I exit our tepee and hold the horses while Father and the other men set snares and fires. The fires force the buffalo to run over a cliff, where we collect them.

NOON: We meet some people from the Arikara tribe to trade some buffalo skins and meat for corn. Mother will be able to make cornmeal mush!

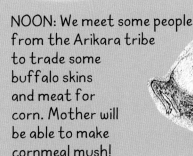

AFTERNOON: Because our morning hunt was so successful, we decide to forage for berries and onions. We are able to return home with many provisions, and then I help Mother skin the buffalo.

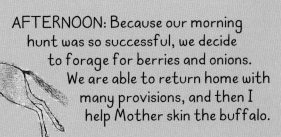

EVENING: The elders tell us stories after a dinner of fresh buffalo meat. My favourite is the story of the Wakinyan, the Thunder Birds, who fought the evil Unktehi, the Water Monsters.

27

# CHAPTER 2

## BONES OF THE SPIRITS

Seth and Luana froze. The Lakota riders dismounted from their glossy piebald stallions.

Luana found her voice and whispered, "Seth! They're the Wild Westers! They're the same guys as on the poster!"

Seth did not care. His eyes were glued warily to the leader of the posse, whose head was decked in a semicircle of long feathers. The Lakota horsemen turned away and whispered to one another in their own language, and Luana and Seth could not understand a word of it.

"Oh, no! We need you, Hiroto!" moaned Luana quietly. "We won't know anything without your translator app!"

A Lakota boy stepped forwards.

"I'm Weayaya, but you may call me Setting Sun. You're lucky – I go to school in Carlisle, where they teach English. I don't like to wear the clothes they've given me when I come home to my people, but I will speak English with you. Who are you?"

"I'm Seth."

"And I'm Luana."

"Well, you have great fortune, Seth and Luana, for my people do no harm to children – even when those children come to steal the great bones of our mother earth."

"We weren't stealing anything," Seth protested.

"We just saw two names on the box, so we thought we might be able to help find the real owner of the bones inside."

"The bones belong to no one. They belong to the spirits of the earth. The best we can do now is to find them somewhere safe to rest. The sheriff pays my people to protect this box. The guards left it for only a few moments to help out in a wagon crash."

"So who are they guarding the box from?" Seth asked, puzzled.

"Hunters and agents paid by Marsh and Cope, of course! We're all hoping that these sacred bones won't get into the hands of either of those two. The sheriff's sick of the trouble they cause. Many bones are transported here by wagon from Como Bluff, where they're dug up. Here they get loaded onto the train. There are often fights over them."

"I didn't think the Bone Wars were that bad!" Seth exclaimed.

Setting Sun explained patiently, "Marsh and Cope are fighting for fame, but for us Lakota, their bone battle is a tragedy. You see, when creation began, the great Water Monsters prowled the Earth. Then they grew cold and attacked other living things. So the mighty Thunder Birds struck them with bolts of lightning and turned them into great beasts of stone. Their bodies lie as stones in places such as the Badlands and elsewhere. Now they are being dug up and broken up in their thousands."

Setting Sun turned to the man next to him, and then to Luana and Seth.

"That's my brother, Mankato. But you may call him Blue Earth. I've told him that you mean no harm. So you can go – they'll join you when the train comes. They're the Wild Westers, and they're off to star with Buffalo Bill. You must want to get on the train, too, for you are dressed to go to town, I think?"

Seth looked down at his dark slim-fit trousers and long jacket, and Luana at her ankle-length, straight skirt and puffed-sleeved blouse. They were certainly not dressed for hard work in the dust of the prairie lands.

HOOOOH! HOOOOH!

A deafening blast heralded the arrival
of the train, turning Seth's and Luana's
heads towards the shining engine.
A wide, fan-shaped cowcatcher hung
in front of it, pushing away debris from
the track. Behind, fancy passenger
carriages, a dining car, a baggage car
and the US marshall's prison truck
with barred windows eased past them.
In the back, a refrigerator car, cattle
trucks and goods wagons clattered and
screeched. Steam hissed and rose.

A loud voice booming through
a megaphone echoed across the tracks:
"All bound for Casper aboard
now! All aboard for Casper! That's
ladies and gentlemen, cattle, chickens...
The other engine's broke so there ain't
no cattle and goods train comin' on
behind today."

Luana, Seth and Setting Sun heard
no more as two men sprinted towards

the box, knocked over the guards and ended up brawling on the ground.

"It's Cope's!" yelled one, elbowing the other out of the way.

"It ain't. It's Marsh's!" growled the other savagely, stabbing the ribs of Cope's agent with a revolver handle.

A Lakota fired a rifle shot into the air, stopping the warring men in their tracks, and two lawmen soon led them away.

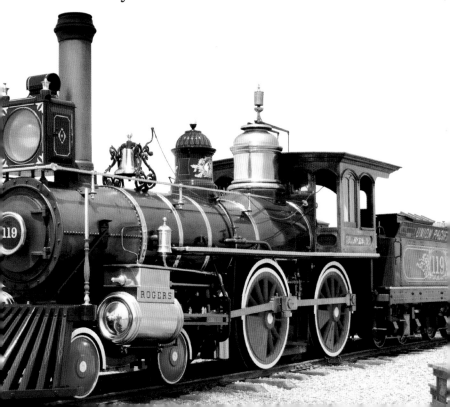

Setting Sun turned to Luana and Seth. "You see our problem now? We need to get this skull out of here and to its rightful owner. That might not mean Cope *or* Marsh. They aren't too proud to take other people's bones."

"Maybe we can call Marsh and Cope on the phone and ask them to describe what's in the box," Seth said. "If they can't, then we'll know it isn't theirs."

Setting Sun roared with laughter.

"This isn't New York, you know! You'll still only find the telegraph here! No. Now that Cope's and Marsh's men know where the dinosaur skull is hidden, we must move it."

Blue Earth bent down from his horse and whispered to Setting Sun.

"My brother says you need to take the box to Casper. Will you do it?"

Luana and Seth nodded.

"Go to the hotel saloon and ask for our friend Gold-Claw Clooney.

He's collecting dinosaur fossils for a museum. Tell him I sent you. I'll be riding over there later."

Luana and Seth scrambled into the baggage car with the box. Setting Sun waved goodbye, but Seth was looking at something else. The great bald eagle that had circled high above them was swooping down towards the railway track. Seth felt uneasy.

Why do you think the bald eagle circling above makes Seth feel uneasy?

# FULL STEAM AHEAD

The building of the railways in the USA was a major factor in bringing people to live in the West. Within a few decades of the opening of the first east-to-west railway in 1869, many towns were built along the railways. Here is one of the locomotives that made this possible.

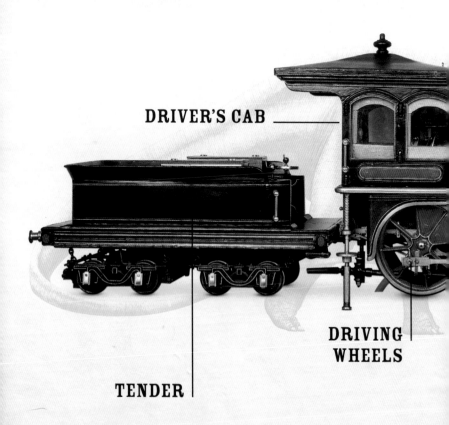

DRIVER'S CAB

DRIVING WHEELS

TENDER

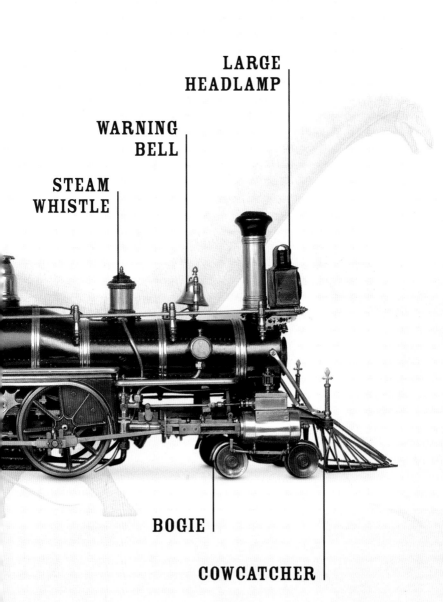

LARGE
HEADLAMP

WARNING
BELL

STEAM
WHISTLE

BOGIE

COWCATCHER

39

# MORSE CODE

There were no telephones in the Old West, so the quickest way to communicate was by telegraph. This was a system that sent messages as electrical signals using a type of code called Morse code.

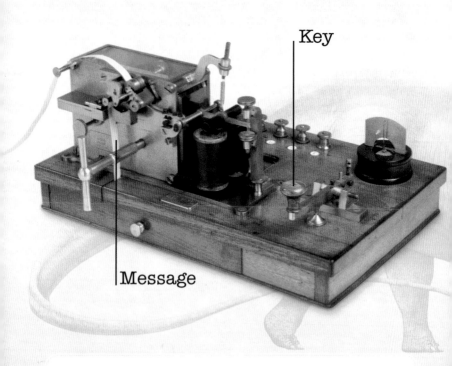

Key

Message

## Crack the code

See if you can figure out what the secret message below says, using the Morse code alphabet opposite.

.--/../.-../-.. .--/./.../-

# How Morse code works

In Morse code, each letter or number is represented by a unique combination of long or short beeps, clicks or flashing lights. Words and sentences are made up by spelling out each word. Here is the Morse code alphabet.

| A | B | C | D | E | F |
|---|---|---|---|---|---|
| · − | − · · · | − · − · | − · · | · | · · − · |

| G | H | I | J | K | L |
|---|---|---|---|---|---|
| − − · | · · · · | · · | · − − − | − · − | · − · · |

| M | N | O | P | Q | R |
|---|---|---|---|---|---|
| − − | − · | − − − | · − − · | − − · − | · − · |

| S | T | U | V | W | X |
|---|---|---|---|---|---|
| · · · | − | · · − | · · · − | · − − | − · · − |

| Y | Z | 0 | 1 | 2 | 3 |
|---|---|---|---|---|---|
| − · − − | − − · · | − − − − − | · − − − − | · · − − − | · · · − − |

| 4 | 5 | 6 | 7 | 8 | 9 |
|---|---|---|---|---|---|
| · · · · − | · · · · · | − · · · · | − − · · · | − − − · · | − − − − · |

The secret message says Wild West.

41

# CARLISLE INDIAN SCHOOL

The Carlisle Indian Industrial School was founded by Richard Henry Pratt in 1879. He thought that Native Americans could save themselves from the hostilities of the settlers by assimilating, which means becoming more like the settlers. He believed this was the only way to save what he thought was a vanishing race.

Native American children had their hair cut short, which for many children was a real trauma. Their long hair was a symbol of their culture, and it was only cut when a family member died. They were also dressed in European-style clothes and were encouraged to forget the language and customs of their people.

Tens of thousands of Native American children attended nearly 150 Indian boarding schools. Some pupils were sent voluntarily by their families or their tribes, but countless others were forcibly sent away to school by government authorities.

Sitting Bull, a Lakota Sioux leader, was against the Indian schools. He said, "If the Great Spirit had desired me to be a white man, he would have made me so... Each man is good in the sight of the Great Spirit. It is not necessary that eagles should be crows."

Here is an example of what a Carlisle advertisement might have been like. What do you think of the Carlisle School?

# CARLISLE INDIAN SCHOOL

## PENNSYLVANIA

Do you want the best
education for your child?
Would you like to live in peace and
cooperation with the settlers?
Then send your children to the Carlisle
Indian Industrial School in Pennsylvania.

At our boarding school, your child will gain the skills
and knowledge needed to live in modern American
society. Children will be taught reading, writing and
arithmetic, as well as a range of craft skills including
carpentry, blacksmithing, cooking and sewing.
The boarding experience of the Carlisle School
will allow your child to learn the customs
and language that will put him on the path
to success in our rapidly changing nation.

# CHAPTER 3

## DINOSAURS IN THE DARK

Seth and Luana settled down in the dim, windowless baggage car, surrounded by boxes, cases and crates. The train was soon rattling along the tracks.

"So, Seth, what's the problem with going home?" demanded Luana.

"Well, the app's confused. It never had fixed landing coordinates, so it just keeps searching. That means we'll never get a fixed point to take off from. We need Hiroto. Let's hope he's got his SLIP app

with him. Anyway, I can't think about it now – I need food! D'you think there's any in these boxes?"

"Oh, honestly, Seth!" Nevertheless, Luana shone her mobile torch on the luggage to keep him happy.

"Here! Look at this! It says '*Stegosaurus* – backbone and tail'. That's the one with the spiky plates all along its spine! And here's '*Coelurus bauri*'. Hmmm. Don't know that one. Do you? We know this one, though! '*Triceratops* – skull and ribs'."

"Wow!" Seth yelled. "But who do they belong to?"

"Well. It's the same story – crossed-out names. Wait a minute. There's a stamp on all of them. It says 'Gold-Claw Clooney'!"

"No way!"

BZZZZZ! Luana's mobile trembled.

"It's Hiroto! I'll read it out: 'Late – sorry guys. Parents say it's a no-gadget holiday! Sneaked mobile out. Need more time 2 identify head. Got 2 go 2 American Museum of Natural History'."

"Is that it?" said Seth.

"Well, he's got parent problems."

The train clanked and shook for another half an hour and then eased up as it pulled into Casper station. Seth and Luana jumped down and lugged their box along the dirt main street, past the few low buildings that made up Casper town.

Luana and Seth stood breathless outside the hotel saloon. The door swung open, and a gleaming gold claw stretched out towards them from a false hand. It was Gold-Claw Clooney.

"Hey! Don't you mind my hand, now," drawled Clooney. "It got blown off in a shoot-out in Deadwood. I tell ya, it was me against ten men, and the only thing I lost was this hand. You should've seen them! Now, I gather from my sources that you are friends of Setting Sun. I also gather that you got somethin' to show me."

Gold-Claw Clooney whistled with surprise at the 'mighty fine head' that Seth pulled out of the box. Then he called out, "Mr Lewis McKay! Would you kindly c'mon out here, please?"

The door swung open from a neat office. A tall African-American man in a suit and waistcoat, his hands full of papers, strode towards Gold-Claw Clooney.

"Now, if you please, Mr McKay, could you kindly tell me what it says on the lid of this box?" drawled the old-timer. "See, I don't trust anyone. Only Mr Lewis McKay. Ain't that right?"

Mr Lewis McKay nodded seriously, saying, "Now guess what, Mr Clooney! This box says it belongs to Mr Cope. Oh, and Mr Marsh, too."

"Weell," drawled Gold-Claw Clooney. "Ain't that just a big surprise? So Mr McKay, if you would kindly log that find in your neat book there, then we'll get our artist to do a quick sketch of that there skull. Records. It's all about records – and evidence. If we don't have 'em, Mr Cope and Mr Marsh will say the whole of America's dinosaur bones are theirs. Now let's get to my bone shed at the back of the saloon here and see if we can match up that skull."

Why does Gold-Claw Clooney need Mr McKay to read the box for him?

Gold-Claw Clooney opened the shed door; inside, dinosaur fossils were stacked rack upon rack and neatly labelled. Great hunks of *Diplodocus*, *Allosaurus* and many other amazing dinosaur finds grabbed his attention, but there was no hope of finding a home for their skull – every dinosaur body had its rightful head.

Disappointed, Gold-Claw Clooney turned to them and said, "Well, I guess you two had better get yourselves to Como Bluff and have a good look there. Ain't no other solution in my mind."

Luana and Seth looked at each other nervously. SLIPs could take no longer than a day. Their mobile batteries would not last, and they would never get home.

"Tell you what," said Gold-Claw Clooney, seeing their anxiety. "There's a ranch just two hours' ride away, where I got me a bone shed. Diggers take the dinosaurs there from Como Bluff. Then Mr McKay goes out to label mine, on the advice of a collector. I get the best of them hauled over here on wagons. Could be the rest of the beast's body is among my bones there. I sure hope so."

He snapped a loose vertebra from the base of the dinosaur skull and gave it to Luana.

"Now, you can't take the whole head. It could be mighty valuable. Try to find the spine that fits this backbone here. And before you go, eat some of these corn oysters and some pickles. Put some beef jerky in your pockets for later. And to show I ain't mean, I'll buy fresh water from a barrel. Casper's got four wells and you'd die of cholera if you drank from any one of them. Oh, and get yourselves out of those mighty fine clothes before someone kidnaps you both and holds you to ransom – 'cos I ain't gonna rescue you."

Seth was overjoyed at the sight of food, while Luana was delighted to pull on some original Levi's jeans, a checked shirt and a real Stetson hat. Clutching a map drawn by Mr McKay and a letter from Gold-Claw Clooney, she mounted her horse and urged Seth on behind her. A loud BZZZZ! from their pockets made them stop in their tracks. It was Hiroto. They needed him badly.

# WILD BILL HICKOK

A tall tale is a story told as if it is true, but in which certain elements of the story are exaggerated, like Gold-Claw Clooney's story about his hand. Here is a tall tale told by the infamous Wild Bill Hickok.

McKandlas was the captain of a gang of desperadoes. One day I beat him shooting at a mark. Well, he got savage mad about it, and swore he would have his revenge on me some time.

It appears he didn't forget me. One afternoon I went out to go to the cabin of an old friend of mine, a Mrs Waltman. I took only one of my revolvers with me, for I didn't think it necessary to carry both my pistols. Well, I rode up to Mrs Waltman, jumped off my horse and went into the cabin.

The minute she saw me, she turned as white as a sheet and screamed, "Is that you, Bill? They will kill you! Run! Run! It's McKandlas and his gang. There's ten of them. McKandlas swears he'll cut your heart out. Run, Bill, run – but it's too late; they're coming up the lane!"

I heard McKandlas shout: "There's Wild Bill's horse; he's here, and we'll skin him alive! Surround the house!"

I looked 'round the room and saw a rifle hanging over the bed.

I put the revolver on the bed, and just then, McKandlas poked his head inside the doorway, but jumped back when he saw me with the rifle in my hand.

"Come in here, you cowardly dog!" I shouted.

McKandlas was no coward. He jumped inside the room with his gun levelled to shoot, but he was not quick enough. My rifle ball went through his heart. He fell back outside the house.

Then the ruffians came rushing in at both doors. One – two – three – four, and four men fell dead. That didn't stop the rest. Two of them fired their bird guns at me. And then I felt a sting run all over me. The room was full of smoke. Two got in close to me. One I knocked down with my fist. The second I shot dead. The other three clutched me and pushed me onto the bed. Then I was wild, and I struck savage blows, following the devils from one side to the other of the room and into the corners, striking and bashing until I knew that every one was dead.

All of a sudden, it seemed as if my heart was on fire. I was bleeding everywhere, and then tumbled down and fainted. There were eleven buckshots in me. I carry some of them now. I was cut in thirteen places.

# WHAT'S IN A NAME?

When a new dinosaur is discovered, scientists give it a name combining Greek or Latin words that describe it. Read each dinosaur name, and then follow the dotted line to find the meaning.

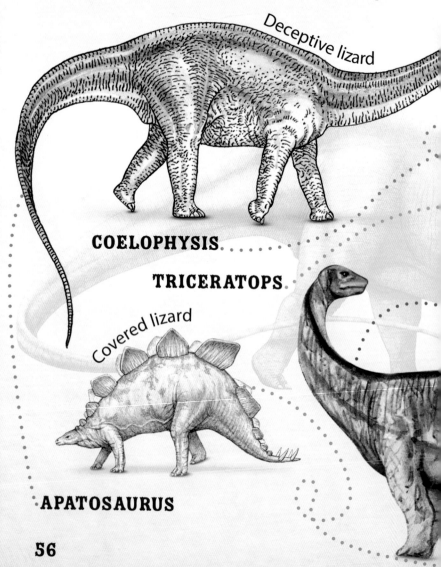

Deceptive lizard

COELOPHYSIS

TRICERATOPS

Covered lizard

APATOSAURUS

# HAT SHOP

Don't leave the house without one of our hats.
Here are just a few of the Stetsons that make up
the best selection this side of the Missouri River!

# BOOT SHOP

We have boots for all occasions, from formal
boots to work boots. Come and see for yourself!

# CHAPTER 4

## BRING ME THE BODY OF APATOSAURUS!

"Are you there? I found your head! It's an *Apatosaurus* – here's a pic to prove it. Things tough here. Had to smuggle my mobile out!"

"Thanks so much!" texted back Seth and Luana.

"Bit of a puzzle," Hiroto continued. "*Apatosaurus* discovered by Marsh in 1877. U r now in 1890. So not sure why your head such a mystery. More research needed."

Seth and Luana cantered on. Just outside Casper's straggled buildings, they came across Fort Caspar. Here, for over 40 years, thousands of wagons had stopped on their journey westwards along the Oregon Trail. People were seeking a better life, as well as luck in the goldfields.

"It's a shame we probably won't see a wagon train," Seth called out. "They'd nearly completely died out by 1890." A while later, however, to his surprise, they came across one at a stopping point by a stream.

A woman called out to them, "C'mon over here and join us folk for some breakfast!"

Seth truly believed that he was still hungry, so he tucked into hot cornmeal mush, johnnycakes and coffee.

"Where are all the buffalo?" asked Luana, looking around her at the cattle grazing on the plains.

"Hunted out," answered one of the men. "This land's either for cattle or buffalo, and cattle win. It's a shame for the Lakota, though. Buffalo are their food, their housing and their clothes." He shrugged. "We understand. We know hardship. This is the second time we've tried the Oregon Trail. The first time, we all got sucked up in a tornado. We don't have the money to go by railway with all our stuff, so we risk our lives and all we have on this trek."

Luana and Seth were soon back in the saddle and galloping across wide,

unbroken prairies. Spikes of mauve beard-tongue flowers rose above carpets of yellow daisies. Brilliant monarch butterflies sucked at nectar from the pink flowers of the meadow blazing star. All around them, goldfinches chatted and shrilled as they pecked happily at ripening grass seeds.

Luana thought they would never see a human being or settlement again but then noticed a landmark to the right of them – a mound of boulders with a kind of wooden cross on it. She knew that if it was the one on Mr Lewis McKay's map, they would soon reach the ranch.

"Here we are, Seth. Let's follow the bridle path eastwards from the landmark, as the map says."

They turned their horses and followed the path until they saw a long, low ranch house stretched across the top of a ridge. Luana and Seth slowed down as they reached a strong gate topped with vicious-looking barbed wire.

A tall man in cowboy gear, but with a neat waistcoat and watch chain, approached them with a frown.

"And just what are you two doing on my land?"

"Are you Mr Johanssen?" Luana asked cautiously.

"I sure am. What you got in your hand, young lady?"

"A letter from Gold-Claw Clooney. It explains why we're here."

The rancher called his foreman, and together they read the letter.

"A mysterious head, huh?" said the rancher thoughtfully. "And you want to find the body? Well, I suppose you can take a look at Gold-Claw Clooney's shed over there. But don't go spyin' on anyone else's bones."

He pointed to the side of the weatherboard ranch house.

"Now, you just wait under those trees and take a drink while I go and find the key to Gold-Claw Clooney's shed. But you say nothin' to those diggers over there about that head, you understand me? It's for your own good."

Seth and Luana approached the shaded trestle table and benches carefully and sat down.

Why might it be for Luana and Seth's own good not to say anything about the skull to the diggers?

"Well. Ain't this nice?" boomed Digger Jaws, who was sitting next to Seth. "We got two young diggers helpin' us celebrate a new name for one of our dinosaur finds. *Barosaurus* – that's what our boss Mr Marsh calls it, and it means 'heavy lizard'. And it sure was heavy. Its neck, well! Seemed as long as a rail truck. And can you believe it only ate plants? I reckon it would've appreciated one of these mighty beef steaks here."

The dinosaur hunters all laughed.

"They say that Mr Marsh himself is at Como Bluff right now, takin' a look at the site."

Luana and Seth looked at each other. Surely they could find a way to Como Bluff and Othniel Marsh? They began to rise out of their seats, but Digger Jaws sat them down again.

"Well, we're done celebratin'. So now I'm gonna tell you nice little children that when you find that missin'

dinosaur body, you come straight back
and tell Uncle Digger Jaws where it is.
Oh, yes, we know all about the head."

Mr Johanssen appeared and led Seth and Luana towards the small, rickety outbuildings that housed the dinosaur fossils.

In Gold-Claw Clooney's shed, Seth and Luana hid behind the door.

"We have to get out of here, and the only way is to SLIP," said Seth.

"Yes, and if we can SLIP to Como Bluff, then we've got a small chance of meeting Othniel Marsh and asking him about the head. But how can we do it when our app doesn't work?"

They looked at each other, smiled grimly and said, "Hiroto! Let's text him! Maybe he can help."

"Tough request, guys!" he texted back. "But sneaked my USB stick out. It's got an emergency SLIP app I use when I help u out from my Kyoto home base. I can only get it to SLIP on a loop. That means u can get to Como Bluff but u have to return to the ranch. Is that OK?"

"Okay! That's genius!"

Seth and Luana knew they would have to face returning to the ranch and the danger of the diggers, though for now, they prepared to SLIP.

Star – hash – hash – hash.

# OREGON TRAIL BREAKFAST

People travelling the Oregon Trail went for days without fresh food. They had to come up with smart ways to prepare food out of simple ingredients that would keep for a relatively long time. Here is a recipe for Oregon Trail johnnycakes.

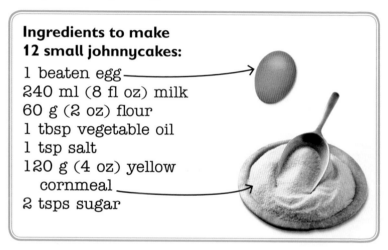

**Ingredients to make
12 small johnnycakes:**

1 beaten egg
240 ml (8 fl oz) milk
60 g (2 oz) flour
1 tbsp vegetable oil
1 tsp salt
120 g (4 oz) yellow
    cornmeal
2 tsps sugar

## Step 1
Combine all the ingredients and mix thoroughly.

### Step 2
Use a tablespoon to drop mixture onto a hot, greased frying pan.

### Step 3
Fry on each side until browned – about 2 minutes.

### Step 4
Serve with butter and syrup.

# OREGON TRAIL GAME

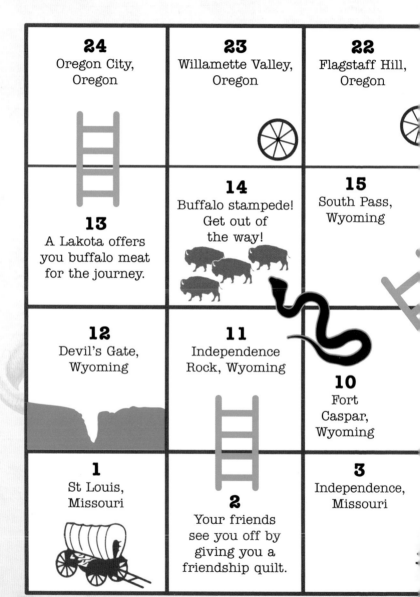

| **24** Oregon City, Oregon | **23** Willamette Valley, Oregon | **22** Flagstaff Hill, Oregon |
| **13** A Lakota offers you buffalo meat for the journey. | **14** Buffalo stampede! Get out of the way! | **15** South Pass, Wyoming |
| **12** Devil's Gate, Wyoming | **11** Independence Rock, Wyoming | **10** Fort Caspar, Wyoming |
| **1** St Louis, Missouri | **2** Your friends see you off by giving you a friendship quilt. | **3** Independence, Missouri |

Take turns rolling a die and moving around the board. If you land at the bottom of a ladder, move up it; if you land on a snake's head, move down. The winner is the first person to reach Oregon City!

**21** The Dalles, Oregon

**20** Someone in your wagon train contracts cholera.

**19** Three Islands Crossing, Idaho

**16** Soda Springs, Idaho

**17** Shoshone Falls, Idaho

**18** A wagon has tipped over in a river!

**9** Time for breakfast!

**8** Scotts Bluff, Nebraska

**7** Chimney Rock, Nebraska

**4** Westport, Missouri

**5** Ash Hollow, Nebraska

**6** Courthouse Rock, Nebraska

# CHAPTER 5

## A MOUNTAIN OF DINOSAURS

Seth and Luana bumped down a stony slope and into a square, man-made pit. Looking up, they were surprised. From a distance, Como Bluff had appeared to be an endless, low, pale-grey ridge. Up close, it was actually a range of horizontal, rocky stripes in yellows, reds and greys. Looking down, Seth cried out, "No way! See here, Luana! Bits of fossilised bone – just scattered! And here! A piece of fern fossil! And a pine cone!"

Luana studied the pit carefully. Small tufts of grass and star-like pink flowers were growing between the loose stones and carelessly tossed bones.

"This pit's abandoned," she said. "Look! Nature's returning. What a mess!"

She took the neck bone from her pocket and examined the jagged remains of abandoned dinosaurs.

Seth shrugged. "Well, we might find a fit, I suppose."

After an hour, they realised that it was a hopeless task. Luana stood up and stretched her back.

"We've only found two other pieces of spine," she grumbled, "and they're totally the wrong shape."

"Shhh!" whispered Seth. "Do you hear that?"

A sudden breeze carried a dull tap-tapping sound from over the ridge. Seth and Luana scrambled up and over. They saw a man working in a newer pit and slid down into it.

"Well, good afternoon!" greeted the man cheerfully. "I assume you've just arrived in those wagons over there?"

Seth and Luana looked over at a fleet of covered wagons and then at each other. They nodded.

"Glad you're not with Marsh's outfit!" said the man with relief.

He was a different kind of dinosaur hunter, Seth and Luana thought.

He wore smart trousers, and his coat jacket and waistcoat were hanging over a shovel handle. He held out his hand.

"Mr Silas Meakin, palaeontologist," he said, "and professional collector of America's finest fossils. I undertake fossil identification and dinosaur reconstruction. Pleased to meet you."

Mr Silas Meakin seemed a trustworthy man, so Luana reached into her pocket for the sketch of the head and the vertebra.

"It belongs to an *Apatosaurus*," informed Seth, "but we've only got the head – the one you can see in the sketch. We were wondering if there was a headless body lying around somewhere."

"Well, the thing is this," replied Mr Silas Meakin. "An *Apatosaurus* can measure 23 metres from top to tail. I think I'd have noticed something as big as that."

He peered at the sketch again.

"You know, I've seen Marsh's *Apatosaurus*, and the head doesn't look at all like this. It's shorter and slopes down towards a wide mouth. And its

teeth are spoon-like, not pegs as
your picture shows. I think you must
be mistaken."

Luana and Seth looked puzzled.
Could Hiroto really have got it wrong?

"And I hate to tell you, but the Bone
Wars between Mr Cope and Mr Marsh
have led to a mountain of missing
fossils, beheaded dinosaur bodies
and blown-up bones."

Mr Silas Meakin explained how
the tale of war between Marsh and Cope
began: "Cope connected up the body
of a dinosaur that he'd received from
a collector in Kansas. But he was in
such a hurry, that he placed the skull on
the wrong end. So the poor *Elasmosaurus*
was stuck with a head at the tip of its
tail instead of its neck! Unfortunately,
Marsh was the one to point it out and
make it public. So from there, the Bone
Wars exploded."

Luana and Seth listened to the incredible tales of outrageous treachery, and with the mobile in his pocket, Seth recorded them all.

"So you see," ended Mr Silas Meakin, "your head could be anyone's, or from anywhere. All I can suggest is that you climb that ridge to the south, where some of Mr Marsh's diggers and collectors are working. But watch your backs!"

Seth and Luana shook his hand and clambered up the ridge. Looking down, they saw a series of pits. They crouched down and watched the hunters while Luana texted Hiroto, attaching the recordings. Much to their surprise, he replied pretty quickly.

"Was about 2 text u! Am in American Museum of Natural History, checking out Cope and Marsh. Stories all true again, and there's more! Head is *Apatosaurus*. Am standing in front of it right now! But it seems there is a story of a missing dinosaur head, too. Text soon."

"Wow, a real missing head! And the Bone War stories are true, too. So those might be desperate, dangerous diggers down there."

"Hmmm. They might be," Luana smiled, "but if we don't go, we'll never know!"

They stepped over the top of the ridge.

"Hey, you! Stop right there!"

They spun around. It was a hunter – with a revolver. Luana and Seth backed down into the pit.

"So! Cope's sending kids to spy on us now, is he? How low can he get?"

"Don't be ridiculous! We're not spies!" said Luana angrily, picking herself up and briskly dusting off her Levi's. "We're admirers of Mr Marsh, and we thought he might be here."

"We're working for an independent collector,

a Mr Gold-Claw Clooney," Seth added, and then wished he hadn't.

Luana stood on his foot and glared at him, and then the hunters closed in on them.

"Gold-Claw Clooney? Well, that makes you spies for him!" said the hunter with the revolver. "So hear this! We're gonna make sure his stash of bones back at the ranch gets a visit. Maybe they'll do a magical disappearing act. And so might you."

His hands reached out to grab Seth and Luana.

"SLIP!" whispered Seth.

With their fingers over the keys of their mobiles tucked into their pockets, Seth and Luana punched in star – hash – hash – hash.

**Why did Seth wish he had not mentioned Gold-Claw Clooney?**

# DINOSAUR HUNTERS

Edward Cope and Othniel Marsh did not uncover fossils alone. Here are a few other characters who helped them make their tremendous discoveries.

## Charles Hazelius Sternberg

An amateur palaeontologist. He and his three sons worked for Cope, collecting fossils in Kansas. The Sternbergs made many great discoveries, including the so-called 'Trachodon mummy', a well-preserved specimen of an *Edmontosaurus*.

## JOSEPH LEIDY

Leidy is known for having named the *Holosaurus* and for realising that it only walked on two legs, instead of four. Cope was one of his students and later became his rival.

# Arthur Lakes

A geologist and teacher. He was hired by Marsh as a fossil hunter after sending Marsh a vertebra specimen he had found. He went on to find remains of *Stegosaurus, Apatosaurus, Camptosaurus* and *Allosaurus.*

# Samuel Wendell Williston

An assistant to Marsh, Williston was known for creating detailed illustrations of Marsh's findings. Soon he began leading his own expeditions and discovered the first fossils of *Allosaurus* and *Diplodocus.*

# HOW FOSSILS FORM

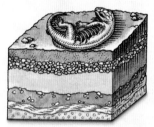

1. The dinosaur dies and its body decomposes, leaving only the harder parts, such as bones (and sometimes teeth).

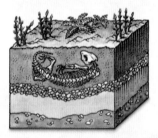

2. Gradually, rock particles, or sediment, cover the dinosaur bones. Over thousands of years, the bones are buried under many layers of sediment.

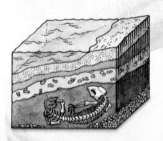

3. The sediment that covers the bones is gradually pushed down to form hard rock. Meanwhile, minerals slowly replace the bones. They turn into rock that is the same shape and size as the bones.

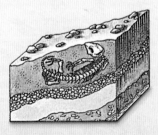

4. Millions of years later, movements in the Earth's crust bring the rock to the surface, where the dinosaur fossil may be discovered.

Como Bluff is part of a geological formation called an anticline, in which the rock layers bend upwards. Over time, the rock in the middle eroded away, leaving two long ridges. The southern ridge is Como Bluff, where the fossils were exposed on the steep slope that faces the ridge opposite.

## FOSSIL FINDS

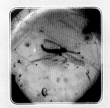

Insects fossilised in amber

Fossilised poo

Dinosaur eggs

# HOW TO MAKE A FAKE FOSSIL

Warning! Ask an adult to help you.

## YOU WILL NEED:

- modelling clay
- petroleum jelly
- objects to 'fossilise', such as seashells or plastic toys
- strip of thin card about 5 cm (2 in.) in width and 30 cm (12 in.) in length
- plaster of Paris
- water
- plastic container

**1** Make a thick, round shape with modelling clay. Flatten the top and smear petroleum jelly over it.

Modelling clay

Object to fossilise

**2** Press the object you want to 'fossilise' into the modelling clay to make your mould. Carefully remove the object without damaging the mould.

**3** Gently push a part of the strip of card into the mould to form a circle.

Strip of thin card

**4** In the container, mix the plaster of Paris with water. Follow the instructions on the package.

**5** Let the plaster thicken, and then pour it into the mould.

Plaster of Paris

**6** Leave for a day to set. Now carefully remove your fossil!

# CHAPTER 6

---

# VANISHED BONES AND BANISHED HISTORIES

"Oooh! Wooah!" Seth and Luana managed to touch down but were immediately sucked back into empty time and space. They could hear nothing and see nothing. Then, with a thrust like a jet engine, Seth and Luana were propelled back down to Earth again, in the shadows between a towering silo and a broad barn back at the ranch.

"Phew!' cried Luana, out of breath. "That was close!"

Seth frowned. "Hmmm." He was worried. Even if Hiroto reprogrammed the temporary app, their SLIP home was going to be scary.

"C'mon, Seth! Cheer up! Let's creep around the barn and listen out for the dinosaur hunters."

From the corner of the barn, they could just see the long trestle table and benches. They were empty. The dinosaur hunters had left along the track towards Casper, and had taken their wagonloads of fossils with them. All Seth and Luana could hear were cowboys – whistling and cracking their whips on the ground, urging a huge herd of cattle into a corral. At the same time, Seth and Luana were looking behind them at a bank of steely-grey clouds towering in the distance.

"Must be a storm coming," Seth said. "They're rounding up the cattle to keep them safe." He shivered at the sight, yet again, of the bald eagle – a speck circling furiously above them.

"Let's just try to find the dinosaur body one more time," suggested Luana.

They made their way to the row of makeshift wooden shacks. The door marked 'Property of Gold-Claw Clooney, Casper' was swinging on its hinges.

As they opened it fully, sunlight hit the roughly hewn shelves and boxes. They were all empty!

"Cleaned out! The dinosaur hunters have stolen Gold-Claw Clooney's finds!" cried Luana.

They picked among the scattered boxes, hoping to find at least some remains, but there were only a few fragments – snapped ribs, broken teeth and crushed vertebrae. Seth and Luana swept them up and placed them carefully into a box marked '*Allosaurus*, jaw bone', which, they noted, was in Mr Lewis McKay's neat handwriting.

"Look at the labels on the boxes!" said Luana. " '*Pterosauria* – right wing, skull, head crest and teeth. No beak'. A flying pterosaur! Fantastic!"

"What about this one?" Seth gasped. "It says '*Saurischia* – skull, left arm and tip of tail'. That's a great lizard-like beast."

"I suppose the diggers removed the bones from the boxes so that no one would recognise Mr McKay's writing on the labels," said Luana. "The hunters will just give them all to Marsh. You know, Seth. This is truly our fault. We didn't have to come here and meddle in the Bone Wars. We didn't have to try to be heroes and solve the mystery of the skull in the box."

"No," Seth agreed. "We forgot SLIP rules. We'd only really researched the Gold Rush, so we shouldn't have become involved in anything else."

A muffled buzz and a jingle from their mobiles made Seth's and Luana's eyes light up.

"Hi guys!" Hiroto's message said.

"Hiroto! Hooray!"

"Hi Hiroto! What have u got 4 us?" Seth texted back.

"Complicated dinosaur story! Marsh was hasty and careless, so he put the

wrong head on the *Apatosaurus* body.
Put *Camarasaurus* head
instead!" Hiroto sent
a picture of the
*Camarasaurus* head.

Seth and Luana
felt a sudden surge
of optimism. Could
their head really
belong to Marsh's
*Apatosaurus*? Seth
texted back quickly.

"So when
did he realise
his mistake?"

"He didn't.
Original head never
found. But an actual
*Apatosaurus* head
from another
skeleton was dug up in Utah in 1910,
after Marsh died. In the end, a dinosaur
expert put it on Marsh's beast."

Seth and Luana looked at each other grimly, and Seth texted back.

"Thanks Hiroto. Bye 4 now."

"You know what this means, don't you?" said Seth to Luana.

Luana and Seth slumped down onto the ground by the empty shed.

"We can't continue with the mission," Luana said miserably. "We can't tell our friends back in Casper that Marsh got the head wrong and that the one in the box would fix the mistake."

"No. SLIP rules say we must never, ever change the course of history. It's so annoying! They'll all have to wait for the 20th century to see the mystery solved!" Seth kicked the dust in frustration.

Luana stood up. "What a mess! A body without a head, and a dinosaur collector without his collection. All because of us."

Seth tried to cheer her up. "Well, we've got loads of dinosaur hunters' tales and pictures of fossils. We also have a great idea of what collectors managed to find. The other SLIP guys will be totally cool about it – especially Musa. You know how he loves digging up bones!"

Luana shrugged. "Let's go and get the horses. They're under the cottonwood trees over there. And then let's get back to Casper."

As Luana and Seth took the reins, their horses reared on their hind legs.

"Wooah!" cried Seth, struggling to keep control.

"They can feel something," Luana shouted. "I can feel it, too. Seth, the ground's trembling!"

The rumbling roared nearer. Then they heard shouting and rifle shots.

"Rustlers! Get your horses and get your guns!" yelled a voice. It was the rancher calling his cowboys. "You two kids! You get yourselves out of here. You understand me?"

Luana glanced at Seth and narrowed her eyes.

"Don't even think of offering to help!" she warned.

The cattle rustlers were approaching from the west. The road to Casper lay due north, but Luana took a narrow track to the northeast.

"The dinosaur hunters will be travelling along the main Casper route," she shouted above the noise.

Seth nodded, and then looked up anxiously, as the great eagle flew fast above them, following them. Seth froze in his saddle, and then took out some beef jerky for comfort. He sensed further danger ahead.

# APATOSAURUS SKELETON

Marsh was getting two different types of Sauropod confused. Sauropods were enormous dinosaurs with very long necks and small heads. See if you can figure out which is the right head.

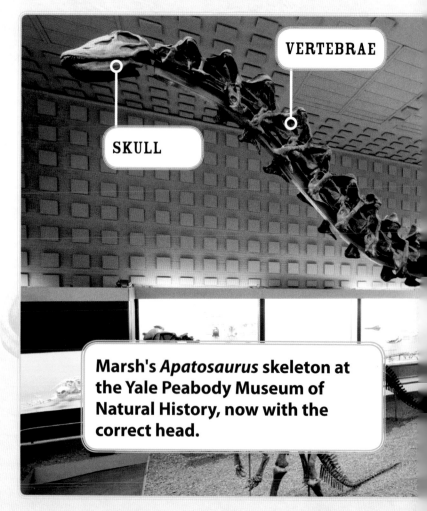

SKULL

VERTEBRAE

Marsh's *Apatosaurus* skeleton at the Yale Peabody Museum of Natural History, now with the correct head.

## Which skull belongs to *Apatosaurus*?

**A**

**B**

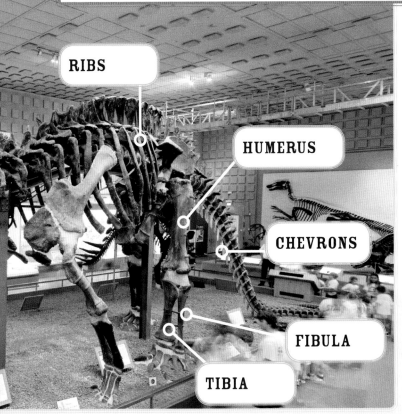

RIBS

HUMERUS

CHEVRONS

FIBULA

TIBIA

Answer: The *Apatosaurus* skull is A.

# SING LIKE A COWBOY

Cowboys in the Old West often had to travel great distances with their cattle. They journeyed for days, or even weeks. To pass the time, they often sang songs. Sing along with this cowboy!

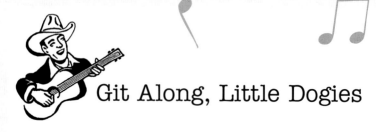

## Git Along, Little Dogies

As I was a-walking one morning for pleasure,

I spied a young cowpuncher a-riding alone.

His hat was throwed back and his spurs was a-jingling,

As he approached me a-singing this song.

Whoopee ti yi yo, git along, little dogies,

It's your misfortune and none of my own,

Whoopee ti yi yo, git along, little dogies,

For you know Wyoming will be your new home.

People in the Old West had their own way of speaking: they had their own accents and special words for things. For example, in this song, 'dogies' are young cows, and 'cowpuncher' is a cowboy. Sometimes cowboys did not speak what we would call 'correct' English. See if you can identify this cowboy's mistakes.

Some fellows goes up the trail for pleasure,
But that's where they've got it most awfully wrong,
For you haven't an idea the trouble they give us,
As we go a-driving them dogies along.

Whoopee ti yi yo, git along, little dogies,
It's your misfortune and none of my own,
Whoopee ti yi yo, git along, little dogies,
For you know Wyoming will be your new home.

# CHAPTER 7

## THE POWER OF THE THUNDER BIRD

"Luana!" shouted Seth after a while. "Above us! The eagle! I think it's warning us about the dinosaur hunters!"

Luana laughed, "No! The diggers are on the other road!"

She turned her head to check out the gracefully gliding bird and frowned. She sniffed the air. It was strange – a bit like freshly mown grass, and then sulphur.

"Seth! Look!"

A great bank of fierce, towering clouds was racing northwards. A slab of dark-grey cumulonimbus stretched out at the top, like wings, while a long column of whirling cloud dipped down

from it – a great
beak pecking
the earth. Shafts
of lightning lit
up the top of
this storming,
thundering beast.

"Like the white
feathers on the bald
eagle's head," said
Seth to himself,
"or a pterodactyl,
or even a great
Thunder Bird!"

"Tornado!"
cried Luana.
"It's following
the Casper road!
But we can't
take chances.
Let's ride!"

As the tornado roared ahead, it sucked up everything in its path. Luana and Seth watched it sweep past them.

"The ranch," Seth said gloomily. "It was right in the way."

"I know – so was the dinosaur hunters' wagon train. I hope they don't get hurt."

"Me neither," Seth agreed. "Let's just hope the tornado missed Casper."

It did. As Seth and Luana tied up their horses outside the hotel, Setting Sun greeted them, smiling.

"I knew you'd be safe."

In the saloon, Mr Lewis McKay was, as usual, clutching a heap of papers. Gold-Claw Clooney sat at a table with a pile of books.

"I've just set up a business in Boston, Massachusetts," said Mr Lewis McKay with pride. "I've come a long, long way from my struggles back down south."

"Before I go, however, I must teach Mr Clooney to read and write."

Gold-Claw Clooney looked completely miserable. He had been trying to read some cheap books without any success.

Luana felt bad telling him, "I'm sorry, Mr Clooney, but we couldn't find the dinosaur body. Even worse, some dinosaur hunters took your fossils from the ranch, and it's all our fault."

Gold-Claw Clooney looked puzzled but then roared with laughter.

"Don't you worry, young miss! I sent for them bones quick because Setting Sun felt a tornado coming. Sad thing was, my men just piled them into the wagons and left behind all those neat little labels. Never mind. Them bones'll all end up in a real museum where they'll get some respect – and so will I. Plus, I'll get a fistful of dollars for my bank account! With all this learnin', I'll be able to write about it, too!"

Mr Lewis McKay stared at him coldly.

"Not at this rate. Pick up that pen!"

Gold-Claw Clooney bent down over his desk, but muttered under his breath, "By the way, I know you kids went to Como Bluff. And I also know that it ain't possible in the time. But I still know you did it. Ain't nothin' gets past Gold-Claw Clooney."

Luana and Seth stepped outside into the cool, starry darkness. Their mobile batteries were dangerously low.

Why wasn't Hiroto texting them?

A sudden thump and a squeal told them that Hiroto had arrived in person.

"Hiroto! What took you so long?" joked Luana.

"What? I've risked my neck for you! Look, I programmed your SLIP return on Mum's and Dad's mobiles and saved them on the memory cards – here!"

As they inserted the memory cards into their mobiles, Hiroto said, "Don't faint, but I actually enjoyed being away from my desk and inside a real museum! I found out a whole heap about Cope and Marsh. You know, they did teach us a lot about our prehistoric past, but it could all have been so much better."

"A bit like our SLIP!" said Seth. "Right! My memory card's in, and I've checked out the app. Are we ready?"

"Ready!" cried Hiroto.

"Just a minute!" called Luana, dashing back into the saloon. She wanted to say goodbye to Setting Sun. She had studied his people's history well and knew that at the end of that year, 1890, there would be much suffering at the Wounded Knee Massacre.

Luana wanted to warn Setting Sun but knew she could not. Instead, she just said, "Take care, Setting Sun, especially... especially this winter. Winters can be hard."

Setting Sun smiled patiently.

"Oh, I know all about this winter. The great twisting cloud that roared like a Thunder Bird told me."

Luana pressed the neck bone into his hand and left. Outside, Hiroto and Seth were panicking.

"I had to set a fixed point for us to SLIP from, and it's right here!" wailed Hiroto, pointing to

the spot where a Wells Fargo stagecoach had just pulled up. Two armed guards were prowling around it, while others gulped down coffee in the saloon.

"Just get your mobiles ready! And, for goodness sake, put that beef jerky away, Seth Trewyn!" Luana ordered calmly.

She crawled under the stagecoach and slipped between the front pair of horses. Rising quietly between them, she yelled suddenly in their ears. The horses reared up, and then bolted down the main street, the stagecoach rattling behind them. Luana dived facedown onto the stony ground, hoping that the hooves and the spinning stagecoach wheels would miss her.

As the townsfolk ran after the stagecoach, Luana stood up. Then together, they touched the keys on their mobiles. Star – hash – hash – hash.

# Lakota Letters

These letters describe an event known as the Wounded Knee Massacre. Some people became fearful when the Lakota began practising the Ghost Dance, in which they gathered in a circle to pray. The frightened people asked for help from the US Government, who sent soldiers to control the Lakota ruthlessly.

Carlisle Indian School
Carlisle, Pennsylvania

20 January, 1891

Blue Earth
Pine Ridge Reservation
South Dakota

Dear Blue Earth,

I hope this letter finds you, Mother and Father well. There have been reports at school about the terrible things that have happened in Pine Ridge. I heard that some soldiers tried to arrest Sitting Bull for practising the Ghost Dance and that somehow he was killed! Is everyone all right? The government officials say that our people attacked soldiers. This cannot possibly be true. It is said that 20 soldiers will be awarded medals of honour for their bravery. I am anxious to hear from you. Please write soon.

Love,

## Setting Sun

Setting Sun

Pine Ridge Reservation
South Dakota

15 February, 1891

Setting Sun
Carlisle Indian School
Carlisle, Pennsylvania

Dear Setting Sun,

There has been a terrible tragedy in Pine Ridge. Chief Spotted Elk feared our people, the Lakota, might be harmed when some soldiers arrived, so he led us to seek refuge with Chief Red Cloud in Pine Ridge. Eventually, the soldiers found us and demanded we give up our weapons. Black Coyote misunderstood Spotted Elk's directions and refused to give up his rifle.

Then we heard a shot. The commander told his men to open fire. We all began to flee, but as I ran away, I saw many Lakota fall. After that, I didn't look back. I hid behind a small ridge. I squeezed my eyes shut and waited for what seemed like hours.

Eventually, it seemed as if the shooting had ended. I got out from my hiding place and looked around. You cannot imagine the horror! Many Lakota lay dead in the grass, including Spotted Elk. It is said that at least 150 people have died. Thankfully, I was able to find Mother and Father, and we are all safe at Red Cloud's camp.

I pray you are well, and I hope to see you soon.

Love,

*Blue Earth*

Blue Earth

# COMO BLUFF AND
# THE WILD WEST TIME LINE

**MESOZOIC** 252–66 MYA (MILLION YEARS AGO)

**TRIASSIC**

*Herrerasaurus*

**TRIASSIC**
252–201 MYA

*Apatosaurus*

**JURASSIC**
201–145 MYA

*Pachyrhinosaurus*

**CRETACEOUS**
145–66 MYA

The times of dinosaurs and cowboys are shown in this time line. Dinosaurs lived millions of years ago, in three periods of the Mesozoic era. The events in this story and everything that has happened since take place in the Quartenary period of the Cenozoic era.

## CENOZOIC 66 MYA–PRESENT

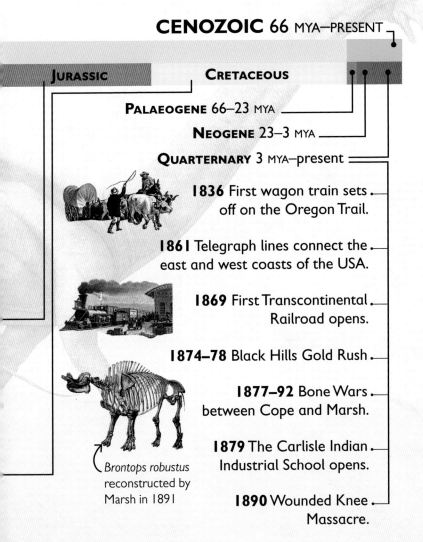

| JURASSIC | CRETACEOUS |

**PALAEOGENE** 66–23 MYA

**NEOGENE** 23–3 MYA

**QUARTERNARY** 3 MYA–present

**1836** First wagon train sets off on the Oregon Trail.

**1861** Telegraph lines connect the east and west coasts of the USA.

**1869** First Transcontinental Railroad opens.

**1874–78** Black Hills Gold Rush

**1877–92** Bone Wars between Cope and Marsh.

**1879** The Carlisle Indian Industrial School opens.

*Brontops robustus* reconstructed by Marsh in 1891

**1890** Wounded Knee Massacre.

# EPILOGUE

"R u back?" Luana texted Seth.

"Yes. Rough landing, though."

"Rough SLIP, really!"

"We failed, Luana. No recordings of old-timers' tales 4 me. Nothing about the Lakota spirit world 4 u. I want 2 SLIP there again."

"U r crazy!"

Seth sighed. Maybe he really was crazy. He sat down in front of his computer and began work on the next mission. Musa, Abrinet and Luana wanted to SLIP back 800 years to the time of the great Aztec Empire in Central America, but Seth could not concentrate. He wandered around outside. He leaned against the fence that surrounded the ring of standing stones and stared at the archaeologists' neat pits. Now part of him wanted to stop it – to let the past and the bones lie buried. He knew deep down inside that his burning

desire for discovery would soon lead him onto another adventure, though.

Over in Brazil, Luana had got over their failure pretty quickly. Sitting at her desk on her uncle's cattle ranch, she looked up at a dark shape that had landed on a power mast at the edge of a corral. To her surprise, it appeared to be a magnificent ferruginous hawk, way off course from its normal range in North America. She wondered if it could have come all the way from Como Bluff!

The bird's great brown wings folded as he shook the grey plumes that crowned his head. Luana suddenly felt something pop up in her brain, like a little bubble of excitement. She strode out towards the mast. Her uncle was there, too, worrying that the magnificent bird would get tangled in the wires.

"Uncle! When are we next going to visit Grandma in Paraná?"

"Soon. Why?"

"I'd like to record her tales of the mysterious mythical giant Blue Crow."

"Our tales, you mean," corrected her uncle. "Luana! Your head is always somewhere else and in some other

century! Sometimes what you want is right here on your doorstep."

Luana giggled. Imagine if he knew that it was not just her head that travelled far and wide and deep back in time!

Deep back in time, Setting Sun asked his brother, Blue Earth, to ride with the *Apatosaurus* skull as far as he could. Blue Earth reached Utah, stopped at a dinosaur dig, and pushed the skull back into the jagged rock. Setting Sun's brother did not know exactly where the head had come from, but he felt in his soul that this was the right place, and so it was.

# DINOSAUR HUNTERS QUIZ

See if you can remember the answers to these questions about what you have read.

1. What is the main attraction in Deadwood?

2. Why did the Lakota move around from place to place?

3. Why are the Lakota trying to protect the fossils from Cope and Marsh?

4. In what year did the first east-to-west railway in the USA open?

5. What was the quickest way to communicate in the Old West?

6. Why can't Luana and Seth SLIP home right away?

7. Where does Hiroto say he will go to find information about the mysterious skull?

8. What does Gold-Claw give Seth and Luana to match the skull to its body?

122

9. Which dinosaur has a name that means 'chambered lizard'?

10. What kind of skull does Hiroto tell Seth and Luana they have?

11. According to one of the men in the wagon train, what happened to all the buffalo?

12. Which parts of a dinosaur are left when its body decomposes?

13. What do Seth and Luana discover when they return to the ranch in Casper from Como Bluff?

14. Who put the wrong head on an *Apatosaurus* body?

15. What does Setting Sun do with the *Apatosaurus* skull?

**Answers on page 125.**

# GLOSSARY

**Amber**
Fossilised material from a plant.

**Corn oyster**
A food made of fried corn batter that is said to taste like oysters.

**Cumulonimbus**
A type of cloud that is dark, dense and associated with storms.

**Desperado**
Someone who is willing to do dangerous things.

**Discredit**
To spread untrue stories about someone.

**Gold rush**
When a large number of people move to a particular place looking for gold.

**Lakota**
A Native American group that lives primarily in North Dakota and South Dakota; they are part of the larger Great Sioux Nation.

**Prairie**
A large, flat area in North America with few trees.

**Vertebra**
One of the bones that makes up the backbone of an animal.

**Wild Wester**
A Native American who performed in Buffalo Bill's Wild West Show; this was a show that depicted stories from the Wild West.

# INDEX

## Answers to the Dinosaur Hunters Quiz:

**1.** Gold – it is a gold-rush town; **2.** They followed the movements of the buffalo; **3.** The sheriff is sick of the trouble Cope and Marsh are causing; **4.** 1869; **5.** Telegraph; **6.** The app they have travelled on has no fixed point to take off from; **7.** The American Museum of Natural History; **8.** A vertebra; **9.** *Camarasaurus*; **10.** *Apatosaurus*; **11.** They were hunted out; **12.** Bones and teeth; **13.** All of Gold-Claw's fossils are missing; **14.** Marsh; **15.** He asks his brother Blue Earth to ride with it is as far as he can and bury it.

# Guide for Parents

**DK Reads** is a three-level interactive reading adventure series for children, developing the habit of reading widely for both pleasure and information. These chapter books have an exciting main narrative interspersed with a range of reading genres to suit your child's reading ability, as required by the National Curriculum. Each book is designed to develop your child's reading skills, fluency, grammar awareness, and comprehension in order to build confidence and engagement when reading.

## Ready for a *Reading Alone* book

YOUR CHILD SHOULD

- be able to read independently and silently for extended periods of time.
- read aloud flexibly and fluently, in expressive phrases with the listener in mind.
- respond to what they are reading with an enquiring mind.

## A VALUABLE AND SHARED READING EXPERIENCE

Supporting children when they are reading proficiently can encourage them to value reading and to view reading as an interesting, purposeful and enjoyable pastime. So here are a few tips on how to use this book with your child.

**TIP 1  Reading aloud as a learning opportunity:**

- if your child has already read some of the book, ask him/her to explain the earlier part briefly.
- encourage your child to read slightly slower than his/her normal silent reading speed so that the words are clear and the listener has time to absorb the information, too.

Reading aloud provides your child with practice in expressive reading and performing to a listener, as well as a chance to share his/her responses to the storyline and the information.

## TIP 2 Praise, share and chat:

- encourage your child to recall specific details after each chapter.
- provide opportunities for your child to pick out interesting words and discuss what they mean.
- discuss how the author captures the reader's interest, or how effective the non-fiction layouts are.
- ask the questions provided on some pages and in the quiz. These help to develop comprehension skills and awareness of the language used.
- ask if there's anything that your child would like to discover more about.

Further information can be researched in the index of other non-fiction books or on the Internet.

### A FEW ADDITIONAL TIPS

- Continue to read to your child regularly to demonstrate fluency, phrasing and expression; to find out or check information; and for sharing enjoyment.
- Encourage your child to read a range of different genres, such as newspapers, poems, review articles and instructions.
- Provide opportunities for your child to read to a variety of eager listeners, such as a sibling or a grandparent.

Series consultant **Shirley Bickler** is a longtime advocate of carefully crafted, enthralling texts for young readers. Her LIFT initiative for infant teaching was the model for the National Literacy Strategy Literacy Hour, and she is co-author of *Book Bands for Guided Reading* published by Reading Recovery based at the Institute of Education.

# Have you read these other great books from DK?

## READING ALONE

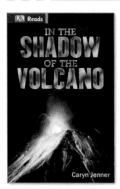

Dramatic modern-day adventure as Mount Vesuvius re-awakens.

Life-or-death futuristic space adventure to find a new home planet.

Pulse-racing action adventure chasing twisters in Tornado Alley.

Time-travelling adventure caught up in the intrigue in ancient Rome.

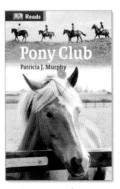

Emma adores horses. Will her wish come true at a riding camp?

Lucy follows her dream to train as a professional dancer.

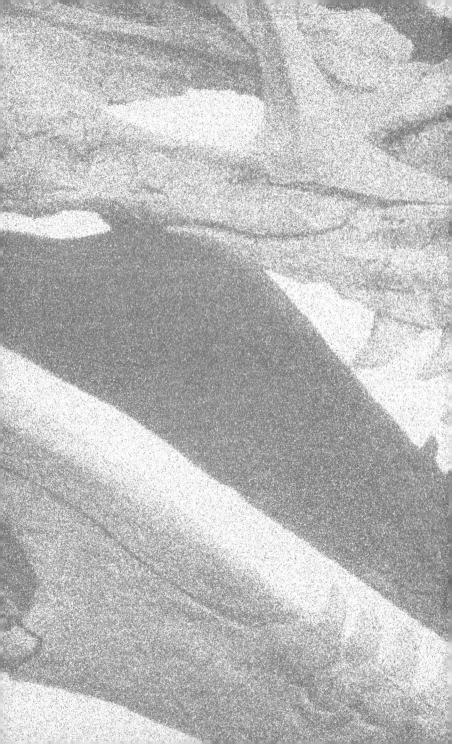